The Story of Creation

Genesis 1–2 for Ch

Written by Beth At
Illustrated by Ed Koehler

ARCH ® Books
Copyright © 1996 Concordia Publishing House
3558 S. Jefferson Avenue, St. Louis, MO 63118-3968
Manufactured in the United States of America

Right from the start of our world God was there—
　　Even before it began.
When He created the planets and stars,
　　He had a marvelous plan.

How did He make it? Well, this is how—
　　Nothing was there to begin.
Darkness and emptiness flowed all around.
　　God *spoke* the universe in.

Planets were set by the sound of His voice.
Galaxies started to spin.
Large ones and small ones all scattered about—
Something where nothing had been.

World without light, without warmth, without shape,
  Like a new seedling asleep;
God's Spirit visited over the earth,
  Hovering over the deep.

"Let there be light," God spoke. It was done.
  Now there was darkness and light.
God said, "It's good," on the very first day.
  He made the daytime and night.

Day two—the waters were split down below.
Spaces were made for the skies.
Now there was water to drink, air to breathe.
All this looked good in God's eyes.

God wanted water apart from the land—
Dry ground appeared on day three.
Water was moved to its own special place.
God called the water the *sea*.

God said, "Let plants appear; let them grow,
    Dropping new seeds as they spread."
Greenery sprang in the sea, on dry land—
    It happened, just as He said.

"Let there be light," God said on the fourth day,
Keeping the day from the night.
God made the sun, moon, and all of the stars,
And they were good in His sight.

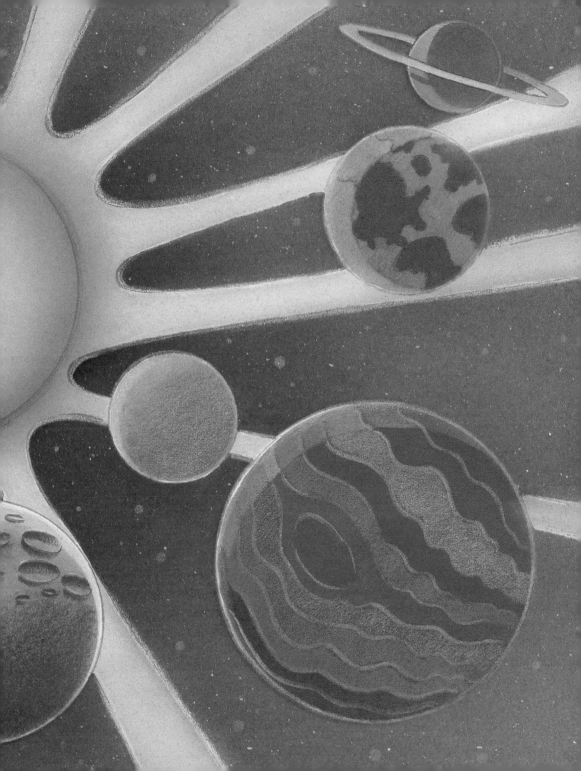

God made sea creatures to swim the vast sea,
Setting the waters alive.
Dolphins and tiger fish, lobsters and whales,
All this was part of day five.

Then God created the birds of the air,
Every winged creature to fly—
Robins and woodpeckers, sparrows and geese,
Flocking across the great sky.

Day six—God made all the four-legged beasts:
Cows, camels, horses, and sheep.
All the wild animals—lions and bears;
All the land creatures that creep.

"Let us make man in our image," God said.
"All living things he'll command,
Tending My garden and naming each thing,
Ruling the sea and the land."

And God formed Adam from dust on the ground,
Breathing into him His life.
God used man's rib to form Eve when He saw
That Adam needed a wife.

God said, day seven, His work was all done.
He made the day to be blessed.
God saw that everything was right and good;
Then He decided to rest.

Adam and Eve kept God's garden with care,
    Tending the fruit and the trees.
God said, "Except for one tree and its fruit,
    You may eat all as you please."

Now, you see, God was right there from the start,
    Planning and building in space,
Making our planet, without life and form,
    Into a livable place.

And from the time you were born, God was there—
    Even before you began.
He gives you His world to love and enjoy;
    It's all a part of His plan.

God keeps you close through the gift of His Son,
Claims you as His from the start;
For the Creator who made the whole world
Creates in you a new heart.

Dear Parents:

Take some time to celebrate and explore God's creation with your child. Make crayon rubbings of leaves and tree bark. Sprout seeds or bird seed on a moist sponge. Look for animal tracks in the snow, mud, or sand, at the zoo or at the beach. Spread a blanket outside at night and enjoy looking at the stars.

Explain that God gives us—the crown of His creation—the job of caring for His world. Plan things you can do as a family—pick up trash, recycle, plant a tree at school or church—to preserve the beauty God created.

Explain to your child that God's perfectly good world didn't last long. It was ruined by Adam's and Eve's sin—and ours. Thank God for sending His Son, Jesus, to die and rise again for us, to restore our perfect relationship with Him.

The Editor